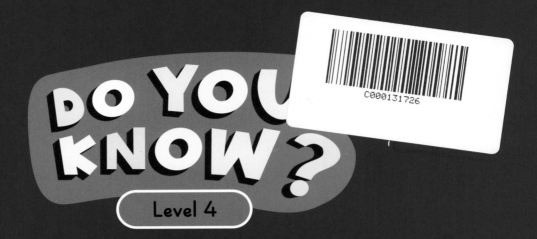

DO YOU KNOW?

Level 4

TINY TECHNOLOGY

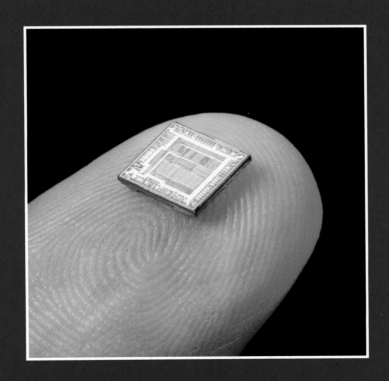

Written by Sarah Shooter
Series Editor: Nick Coates
Designed by Dynamo Limited

LADYBIRD BOOKS

UK | USA | Canada | Ireland | Australia
India | New Zealand | South Africa

Ladybird Books Ltd is part of the Penguin Random House group of companies
whose addresses can be found at global.penguinrandomhouse.com.
www.penguin.co.uk   www.puffin.co.uk   www.ladybird.co.uk

Penguin
Random House
UK

First published 2022
001

Text copyright © Ladybird Books Ltd, 2022

Printed in China

The authorized representative in the EEA is Penguin Random House Ireland,
Morrison Chambers, 32 Nassau Street, Dublin D02 YH68

A CIP catalogue record for this book is available from the British Library

ISBN: 978-0-241-55949-9

All correspondence to:
Ladybird Books
Penguin Random House Children's
One Embassy Gardens, 8 Viaduct Gardens, London SW11 7BW

Contents

New words

accurate

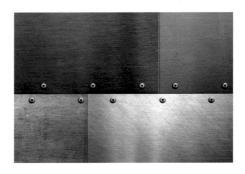

information

measure

metal

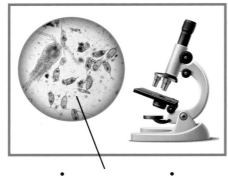

microscopic

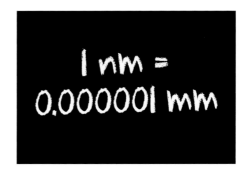

nanometre

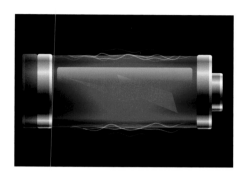

power

scientist

split

tiny

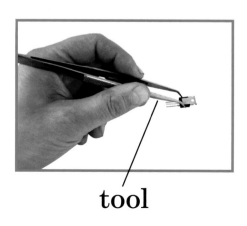

tool

What is tiny technology?

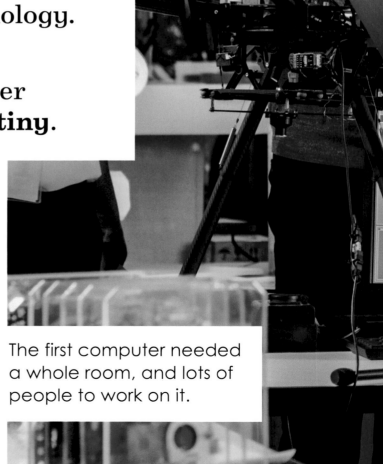

Science is the study of the world to understand it better. We use what we learn from science to make things that make our lives better. We call these things technology.

When technology gets better, it can get smaller and smaller. It can be **tiny**.

The first computer needed a whole room, and lots of people to work on it.

Now, we can do the same things with a laptop at home!

This is one of the smallest computers in the world.

THINK!

Can you think of any tiny technology?
Is there tiny technology in your school?

Why does technology get smaller?

Scientists try to make new and better **tools**. When tools are better, they can be more **accurate**. With very accurate tools, we can make very small things.

Better batteries can hold more **power** – even when they're tiny.

battery

library

SD card

This SD card is tiny. It can hold more **information** than a library!

🔍 LOOK!

Look at the pages.
Which is bigger here: the SD card or the finger?

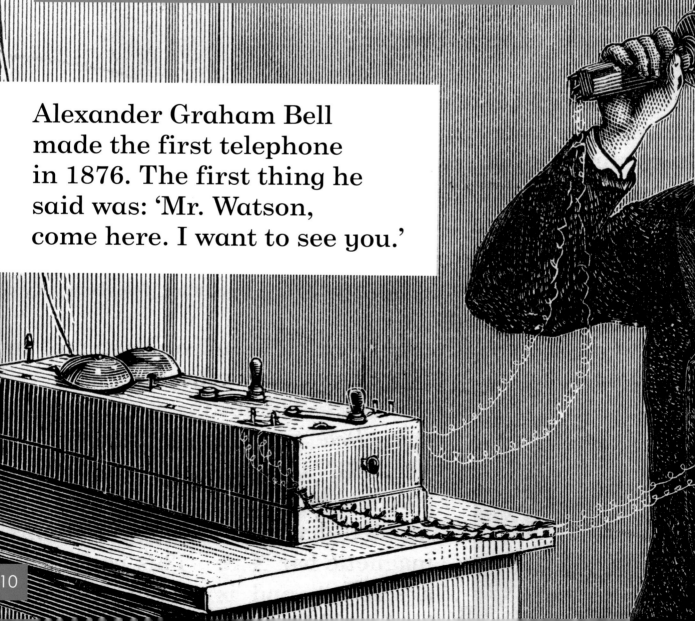

When did technology become tiny?

Alexander Graham Bell made the first telephone in 1876. The first thing he said was: 'Mr. Watson, come here. I want to see you.'

This is a mobile phone from 1984. It had a big battery, and was very heavy!

In the 1990s and 2000s, mobile phones became smaller and smaller.

Today, we like our mobile phones to be bigger. We want to watch films on them, or make video calls. But they aren't too big. They can go in our pockets, too.

🔍 LOOK!

Look at the pages.
How are old phones different from new phones?
How many buttons do they have?

How big is a camera?

We use cameras for taking photos. We see lots of photos every day, but how do we make them?

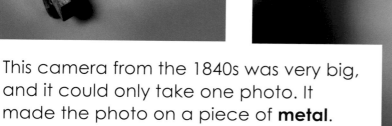

This camera from the 1840s was very big, and it could only take one photo. It made the photo on a piece of **metal**.

With better technology, cameras got smaller. They needed film to take photos. Photos from film were made in a darkroom.

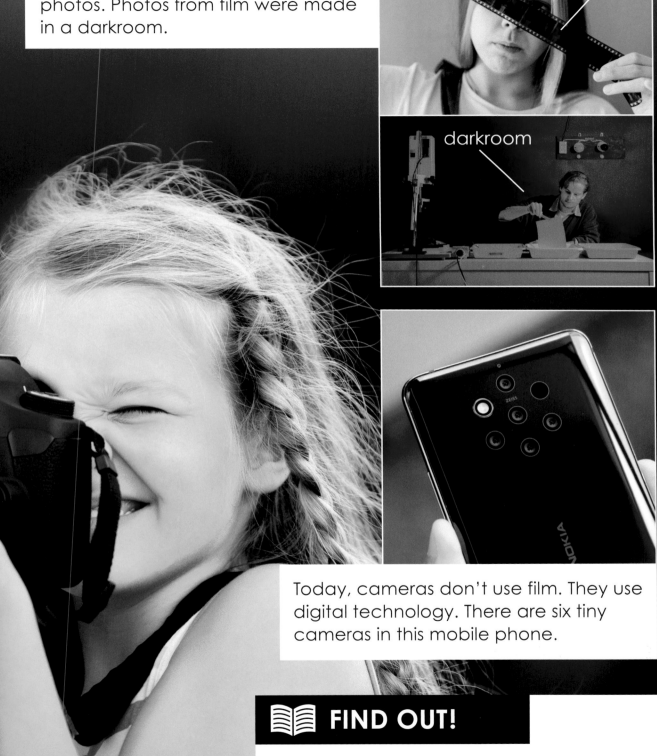

film

darkroom

Today, cameras don't use film. They use digital technology. There are six tiny cameras in this mobile phone.

📖 FIND OUT!

Use books or the internet to find out what cameras in phones are made of.

Was there tiny technology in the past?

Clockwork technology is very old – more than 2,000 years old! Clockwork uses metal gears. Some gears are large, and some are tiny. In the 1300s, people started to make clocks with clockwork.

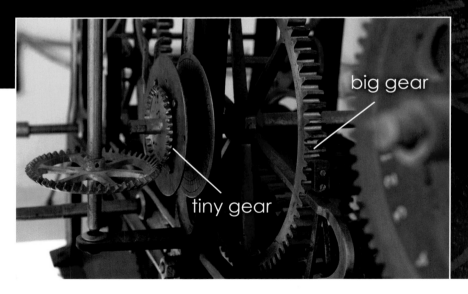

big gear

tiny gear

The big gear in a clock turns once every hour. It turns 24 times in one day. The tiny gears turn faster.

tiny spring

clockwork

From around 1450, clockwork started to use a spring. This spring is tiny.

Clockwork is not only for clocks. Toys use tiny clockwork, too. This box plays music and things move!

▶ **WATCH!**

Watch the video (see page 32).
Can you see the gears moving?
What are they doing?

What is a microchip?

Most technology today has microchips in it. Computers, cars, fridges and toothbrushes can all have them.

microchip

A microchip is very small, but it can do lots of things. It has lots of tiny parts that use and send information.

Microchips help scientists to make very fast computers. This type of microchip uses lots of information.

Pets can have microchips, too! If you lose your dog, a microchip helps you to find them.

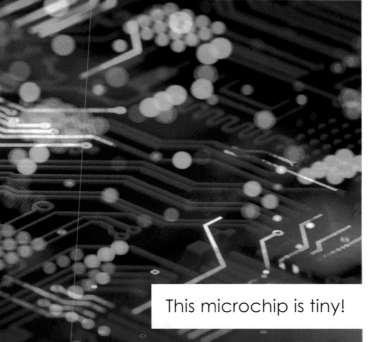

This microchip is tiny!

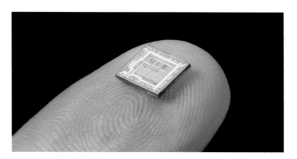

📖 FIND OUT!

Use books or the internet to find out if phones have microchips.

What does a microscope do?

We use a microscope to look at very small things. It can show us things that we can't see with only our eyes. We call things that we can't see with our eyes **microscopic**.

microscope

cells

This is an onion. If you look through a microscope, you can see the cells of the onion.

This is microscopic bacteria from a yoghurt. If you look through the microscope, you can see the bacteria move.

bacteria

cheek

yoghurt

cheek cells

These are cells from a person's cheek under a microscope!

▶ **WATCH!**

Watch the video (see page 32).
What can you see through the microscope?

This is sand from a beach under a microscope. Sand isn't microscopic, but we can see it better with a microscope.

Microscopes are awesome . . .
but do you know that they use the
same technology as a pair of glasses?

Glasses help us to see.

lens

This is a magnifying glass. When you look through it, you can see small things better.

A microscope has two or more lenses. Now we can see things that are smaller and smaller.

📖 **FIND OUT!**

Use books or the internet. A microscope helps us to see small things. What helps us to see things that are far away? Does it use lenses?

21

How long is a nanometre?

We use **nanometres** to **measure** things that are very, very small. You need a very strong microscope to see 1 nanometre, because it is so tiny.

There are 10 million nanometres in 1 centimetre.

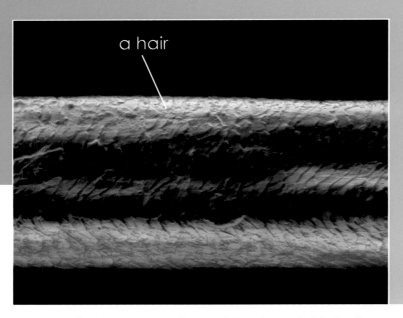

a hair

One hair from your head is about 80,000 nanometres wide.

A sheet of paper is around 100,000 nanometres thick.

This ant is about 5 million nanometres long. That's half a centimetre!

📖 FIND OUT!

Use a ruler. Measure something very small. How many nanometres is it?

What is nanotechnology?

Some scientists study and make technology with things smaller than 100 nanometres. This is called nanotechnology.

Scientists use a very strong microscope to work with this tiny technology!

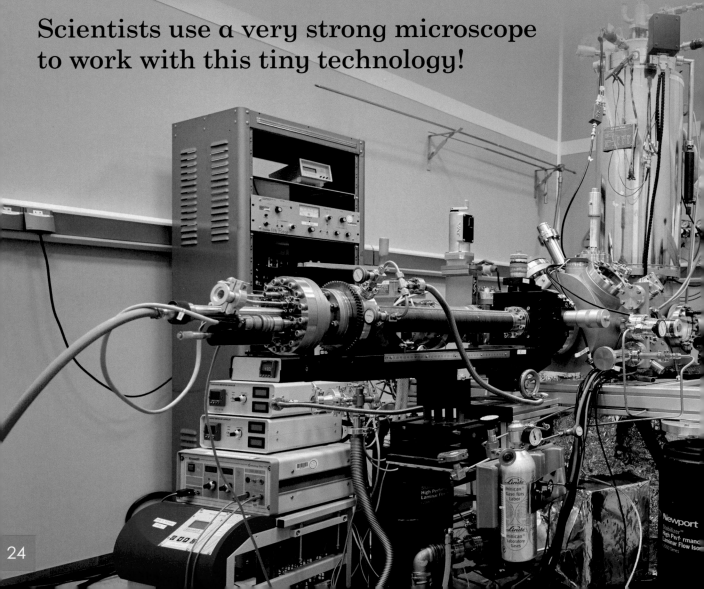

This is a carbon nanotube. It is about one nanometre wide, but it is very strong.

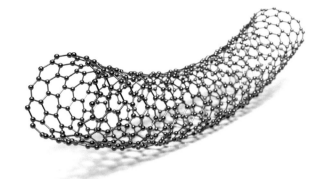

Scientists are trying to put nanotechnology into contact lenses. In the future, we may make and play videos using only contact lenses!

contact lens

sun cream

Today, some sun creams use nanotechnology. They have tiny pieces of metal to keep away the light from the sun.

THINK!

Is a carbon nanotube bigger than a hair from your head?

How small is the smallest robot?

Robots can do important jobs for us. With nanotechnology, we can make tiny robots. A robot that is only a few thousand nanometres is a nanobot.

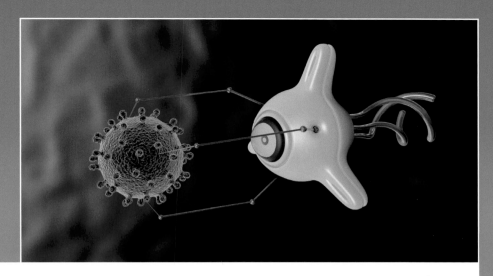

This is a nanobot. When you are ill, this nanobot can take medicine to the right place in your body!

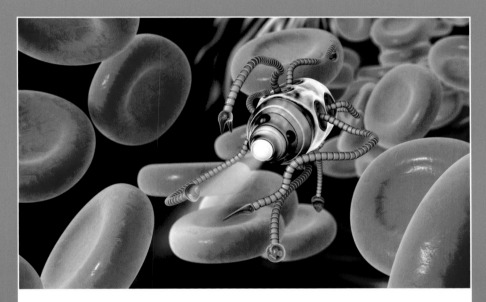

In the future, nanobots may travel around our body and find problems before we feel ill.

 **PROJECT**

Work with a friend. Draw your own tiny robot. What can it do?

27

What is smaller than a nanometre?

Everything in the world is made of atoms. Atoms are tiny. There are about ten atoms in a nanometre.

atom

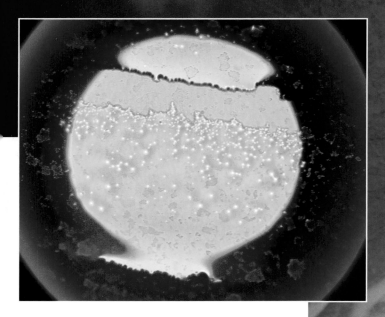

You can use a very strong microscope to look at atoms.

When you **split** some types of atoms in two, they get very hot. Scientists use this technology to make power for our cities.

This is the Large Hadron Collider in Switzerland. Scientists use it to look for things that are smaller than an atom!

 **FIND OUT!**

Use books or the internet. What are the three parts of an atom called?

Quiz

Choose the correct answers.

1 Science is the study of . . .

a computers.

b the world.

c tiny things.

2 The first . . . was made in 1876.

a bell

b battery

c telephone

3 Cameras in the 1840s were very . . .

a dangerous.

b small.

c big.

4 Computers, cars and fridges have . . .

a microchips.

b microscopes.

c mobile phones.

5 You can only see . . . with a microscope.

   a bacteria

   b an onion

   c yoghurt

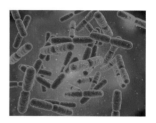

6 How many nanometres wide is one hair?

   a 1 nanometre

   b 80,000 nanometres

   c 5 million nanometres

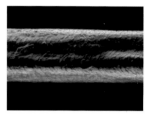

7 A carbon nanotube is very . . .

   a big.

   b strong.

   c heavy.

8 When you split an atom, it gets . . .

   a very hot.

   b very cold.

   c very green.

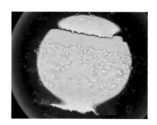

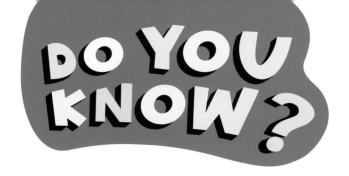

Visit www.ladybirdeducation.co.uk for FREE DO YOU KNOW? teaching resources.

- video clips with simplified voiceover and subtitles
- video and comprehension activities
- class projects and lesson plans
- audio recording of every book
- digital version of every book
- full answer keys

To access video clips, audio tracks and digital books:

1 Go to **www.ladybirdeducation.co.uk**
2 Click 'Unlock book'
3 Enter the code below

02UeIhNno1

Stay safe online! Some of the DO YOU KNOW? activities ask children to do extra research online. Remember:

- ensure an adult is supervising;
- use established search engines such as Google or Kiddle;
- children should never share personal details, such as name, home or school address, telephone number or photos.